WITHDRAWN
FROM THE RECORDS OF THE
MID-CONTINENT PUBLIC LI
NO
D1175437

Compass Point

Phonics Readers

Can You See It?

by Wiley Blevins

Reading Consultant: Wiley Blevins, M.A.
Phonics/Early Reading Specialist

COMPASS POINT BOOKS

Minneapolis, Minnesota

Compass Point Books
3109 West 50th Street, #115
Minneapolis, MN 55410

Visit Compass Point Books on the Internet at *www.compasspointbooks.com*
or e-mail your request to *custserv@compasspointbooks.com*

Photographs ©: Cover: Dave Welling Photography, p. 1: Dave Welling Photography, p. 6: Folio, Inc./David R. Frazier, p. 7: Photo Researchers, Inc./Steve Maslowski, p. 8: Photo Researchers, Inc./Rod Planck, p. 9: Minden Pictures/Thomas Mangelsen, p. 10: Bruce Coleman, Inc./Jane Burton, p. 11: Minden Pictures/Michael Quinton, p. 12: Photo Researchers, Inc./David Hall

Editorial Development: Alice Dickstein, Alice Boynton
Photo Researcher: Wanda Winch
Design/Page Production: Silver Editions, Inc.

Library of Congress Cataloging-in-Publication Data

Blevins, Wiley.
Can you see it? / by Wiley Blevins.
p. cm. — (Compass Point phonics readers)
Summary: Invites the reader to look for animals hidden or camouflaged in the pictures, while reading a text that incorporates phonics instruction and rebuses.
Includes bibliographical references and index.
ISBN 0-7565-0506-2 (hardcover : alk. paper)
1. Animals—Juvenile literature. 2. Reading—Phonetic method—Juvenile literature. [1. Animals. 2. Picture puzzles. 3. Rebuses. 4. Reading—Phonetic method.] I. Title. II. Series.
QL49.B637 2003
590—dc21 2003006350

Table of Contents

Dear Parent or Caregiver,

Welcome to Compass Point Phonics Readers, books of information for young children. Each book concentrates on specific phonic sounds and words commonly found in beginning reading materials. Featuring eye-catching photographs, every book explores a single science or social studies concept that is sure to grab a child's interest.

So snuggle up with your child, and let's begin. Start by reading aloud the Mother Goose nursery rhyme on the next page. As you read, stress the words in dark type. These are the words that contain the phonic sounds featured in this book. After several readings, pause before the rhyming words, and let your child chime in.

Now let's read *Can You See It?* If your child is a beginning reader, have him or her first read it silently. Then ask your child to read it aloud. For children who are not yet reading, read the book aloud as you run your finger under the words. Ask your child to imitate, or "echo," what he or she has just heard.

Discussing the book's content with your child:
Explain to your child that animals may be camouflaged through their natural coloring (an arctic fox), by changing colors (a chameleon), or by their shape that allows them to blend in with their surroundings (a praying mantis or the owl on the cover of the book).

At the back of the book is a fun Batter Up! game. Your child will take pride in demonstrating his or her mastery of the phonic sounds and the high-frequency words.

Enjoy Compass Point Phonics Readers and watch your child read and learn!

Lizabeth

Lizabeth, Lissy, **Betsy,** and **Bess,**
They all **went** together to seek
a bird's **nest.**
They found a bird's **nest** with
five **eggs** in,
They all took one and **left** four in.

A big bug is on a 

.
Can you see it?

A red bird is in a 

.
Can you see it?

A lizard is on a wet rock.
Can you see it?

A big tiger is in the grass.
Can you see it?

A crab went in a shell.
Can you see it?

A rabbit rests in a log.
Can you see it?

Can you see 2 red 

?
Yes I can!

Word List

Short *e*

red

rests

went

wet

yes

***r*-Blends**

crab

grass

High-Frequency

you

Science

bird

bug

Batter Up!

You will need:

- 1 penny
- 2 moving pieces, such as nickels or checkers

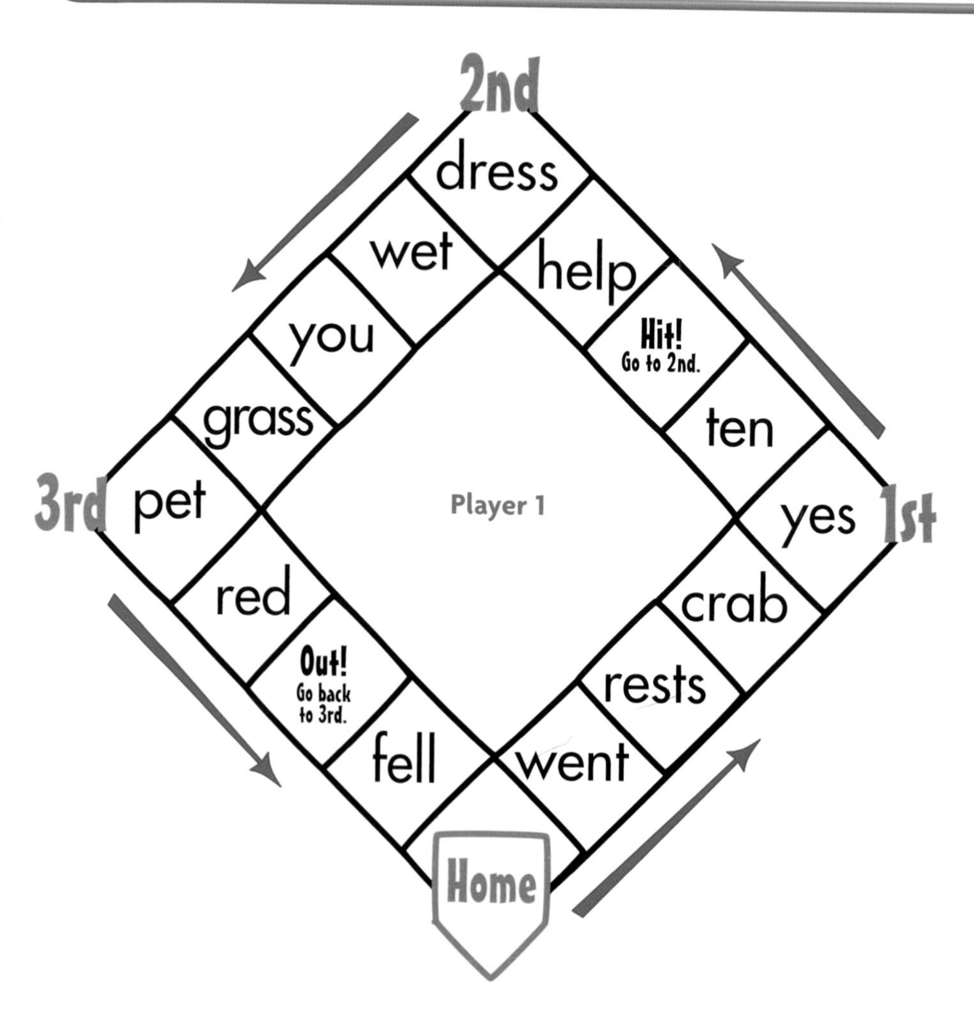

How to Play

- Put the moving pieces on Home. The first player shakes the penny and drops it on the table. Heads means move 1 space. Tails means move 2 spaces.
- The player moves and reads the word. If the child does not read the word correctly, tell him or her what it is. On the next turn, the child must read the word before moving.
- A run is scored by the first player to arrive at Home plate, and the inning is over. Continue playing out the number of innings previously decided. The player with the most runs wins.

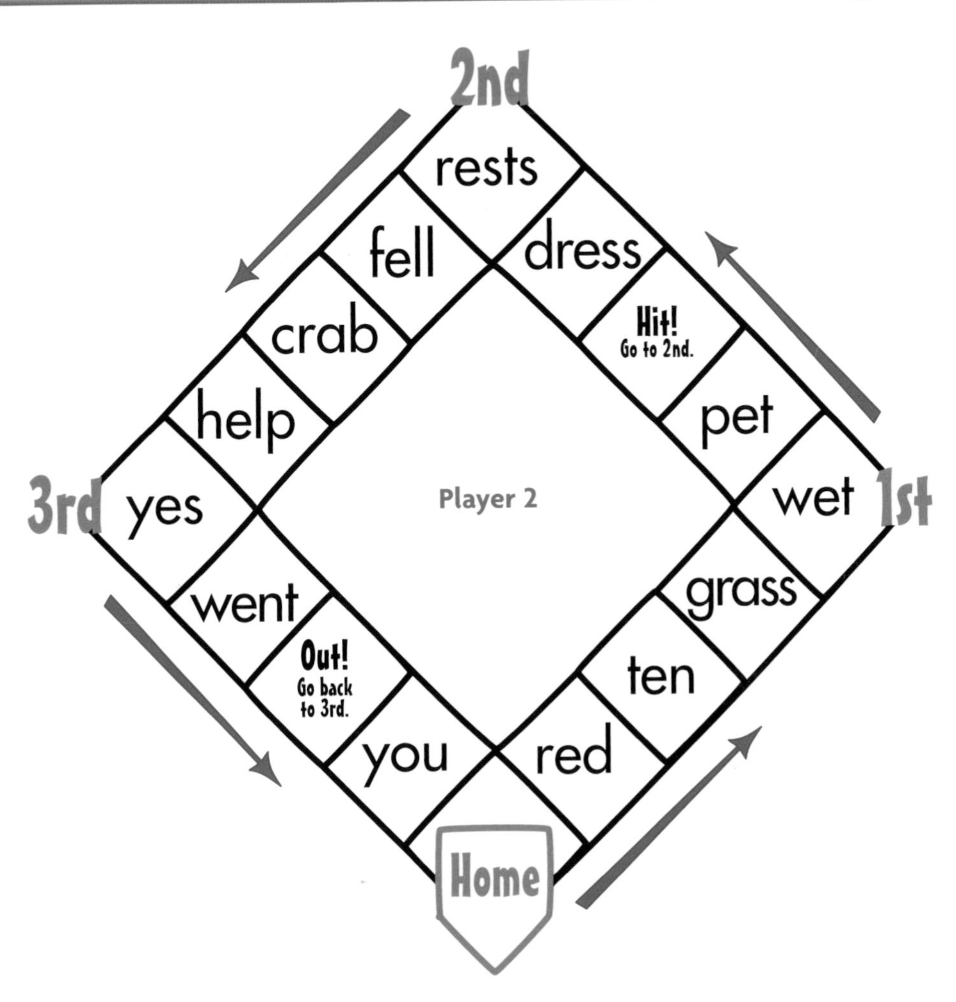

Read More

Frost, Helen. *Butterfly Colors.* Mankato, Minn.: Pebble Books, 1999.

Frost, Helen. *Walkingsticks.* Mankato, Minn.: Pebble Books, 2001.

Whitehouse, Patricia. *Hiding in a Desert*. Chicago, Ill.: Heinemann Library, 2003.

Whitehouse, Patricia. *Hiding in the Ocean*. Chicago, Ill.: Heinemann Library, 2003.

Index